Guest book to celebrate

Gallery of friends

Happy thoughts......

_____

_____

_____

_____

_____

Name _____

♥ *Email/Phone* _____

Happy thoughts......

_____

_____

_____

_____

_____

Name _____

♥ *Email/Phone* _____

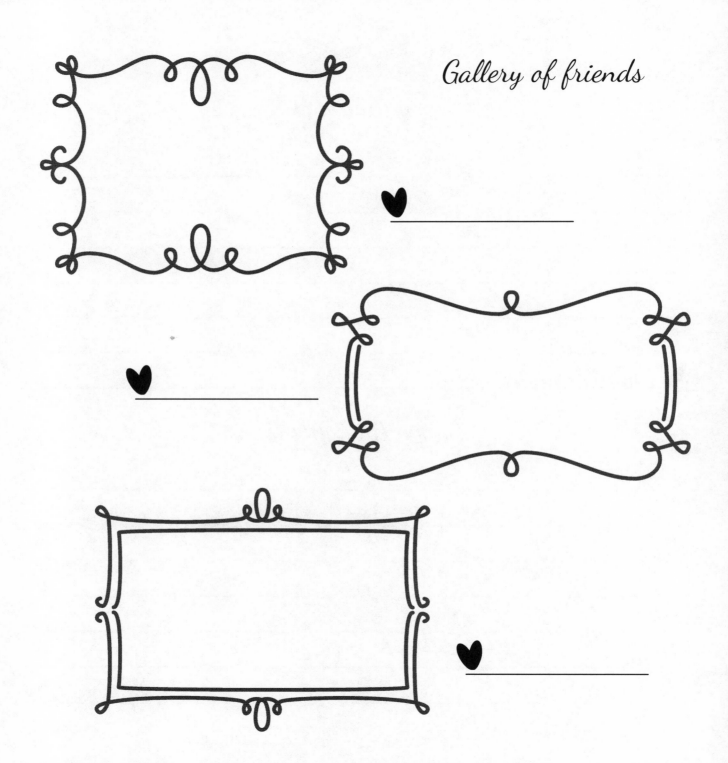

Gallery of friends

Happy thoughts......

_____

_____

_____

_____

_____

Name _____

♥ Email/Phone _____

Happy thoughts......

_____

_____

_____

_____

Name _____

♥ Email/Phone _____

Gallery of friends

Happy thoughts......

_____

_____

_____

_____

<u>Name</u>

♥ *Email/Phone*

Happy thoughts......

_____

_____

_____

_____

<u>Name</u>

♥ *Email/Phone*

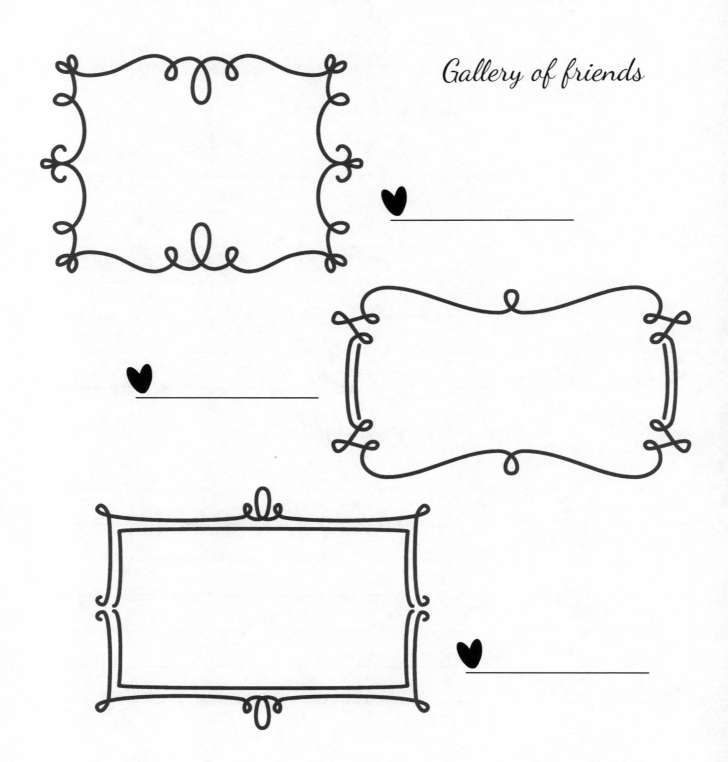

Gallery of friends

Happy thoughts......

_____

_____

_____

_____

_____

Name _____

♥ *Email/Phone* _____

Happy thoughts......

_____

_____

_____

_____

_____

Name _____

♥ *Email/Phone* _____

Gallery of friends

Happy thoughts......

_____

_____

_____

_____

_____

<u>Name</u>

♥ *Email/Phone* _____

Happy thoughts......

_____

_____

_____

_____

_____

<u>Name</u>

♥ *Email/Phone* _____

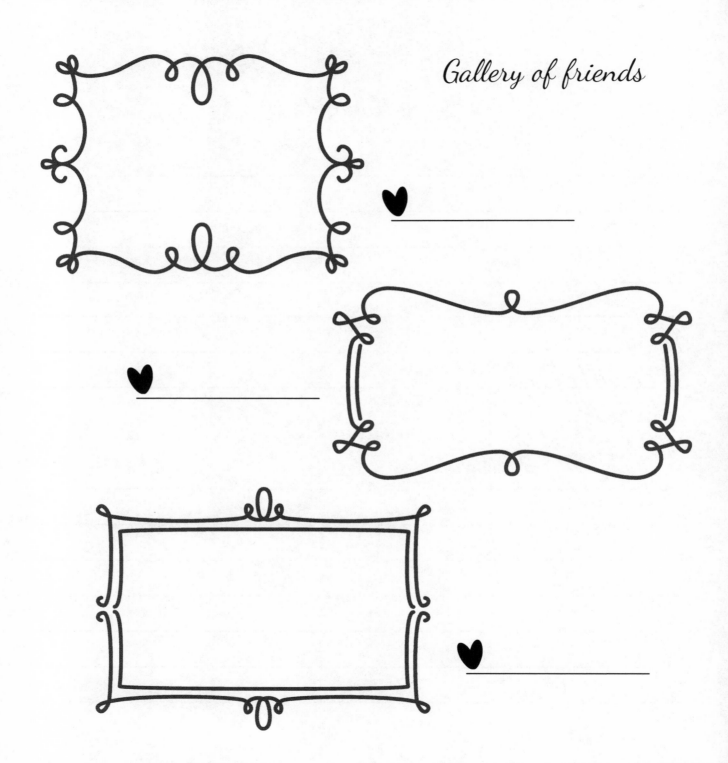

Gallery of friends

Happy thoughts......

_____

_____

_____

_____

_____

<u>Name</u>
♥ *Email/Phone*

Happy thoughts......

_____

_____

_____

_____

_____

<u>Name</u>
♥ *Email/Phone*

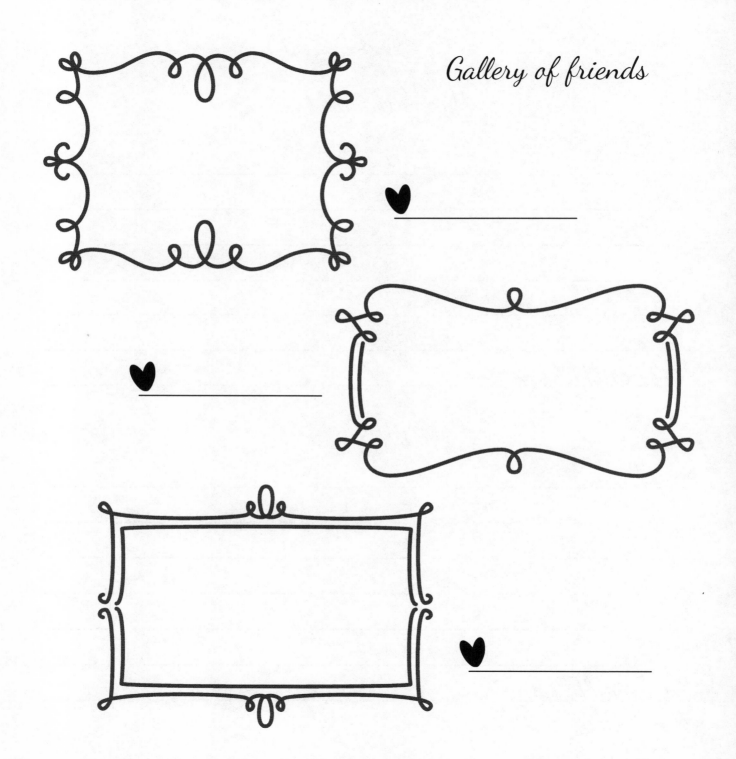

Gallery of friends

Happy thoughts......

_____
_____
_____
_____
_____

Name _____
♥ Email/Phone _____

Happy thoughts......

_____
_____
_____
_____
_____

Name _____
♥ Email/Phone _____

Gallery of friends

Happy thoughts......

_____

_____

_____

_____

_____

<u>Name</u> _____

♥ <u>Email/Phone</u> _____

Happy thoughts......

_____

_____

_____

_____

_____

<u>Name</u> _____

♥ <u>Email/Phone</u> _____

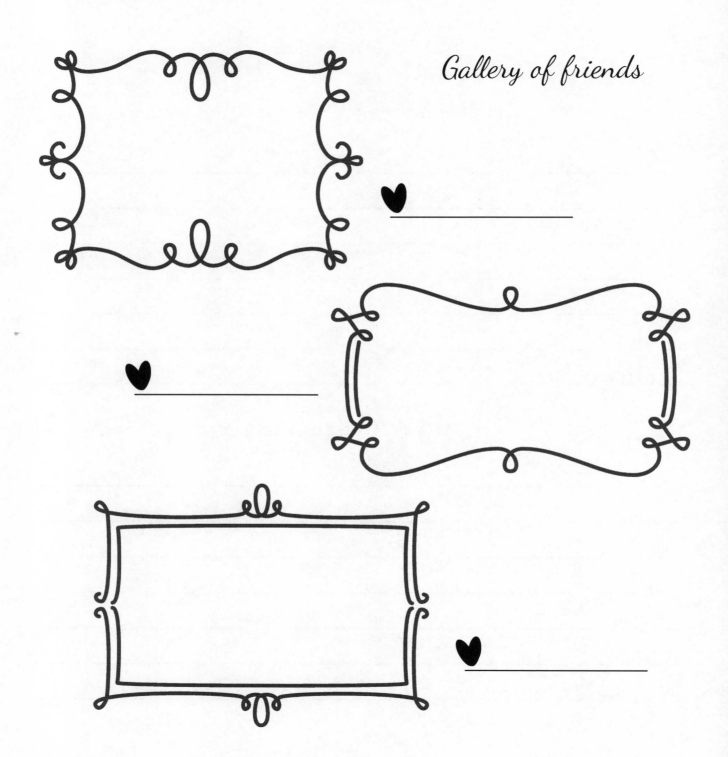

Gallery of friends

Happy thoughts......

_____

_____

_____

_____

_____

<u>*Name*</u>

♥ <u>*Email/Phone*</u> _____

Happy thoughts......

_____

_____

_____

_____

_____

<u>*Name*</u>

♥ <u>*Email/Phone*</u> _____

Gallery of friends

Happy thoughts......

_____

_____

_____

_____

_____

<u>*Name*</u>

♥ *Email/Phone* _____

Happy thoughts......

_____

_____

_____

_____

_____

<u>*Name*</u>

♥ *Email/Phone* _____

Gallery of friends

Happy thoughts......

_____

_____

_____

_____

<u>Name</u>_____

♥ *Email/Phone*_____

Happy thoughts......

_____

_____

_____

_____

<u>Name</u>_____

♥ *Email/Phone*_____

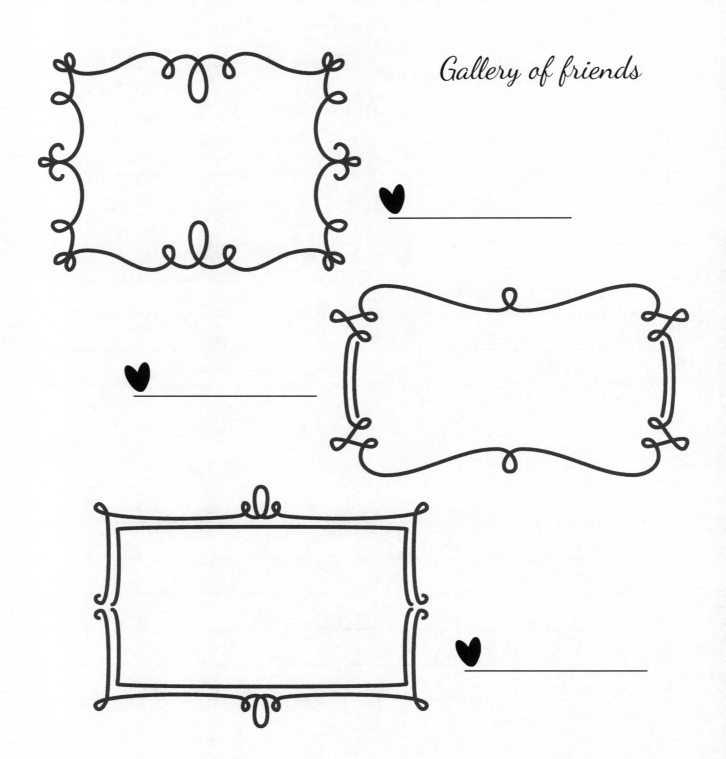

Gallery of friends

Happy thoughts......

_____

_____

_____

_____

<u>Name</u> _____

♥ <u>Email/Phone</u> _____

Happy thoughts......

_____

_____

_____

_____

<u>Name</u> _____

♥ <u>Email/Phone</u> _____

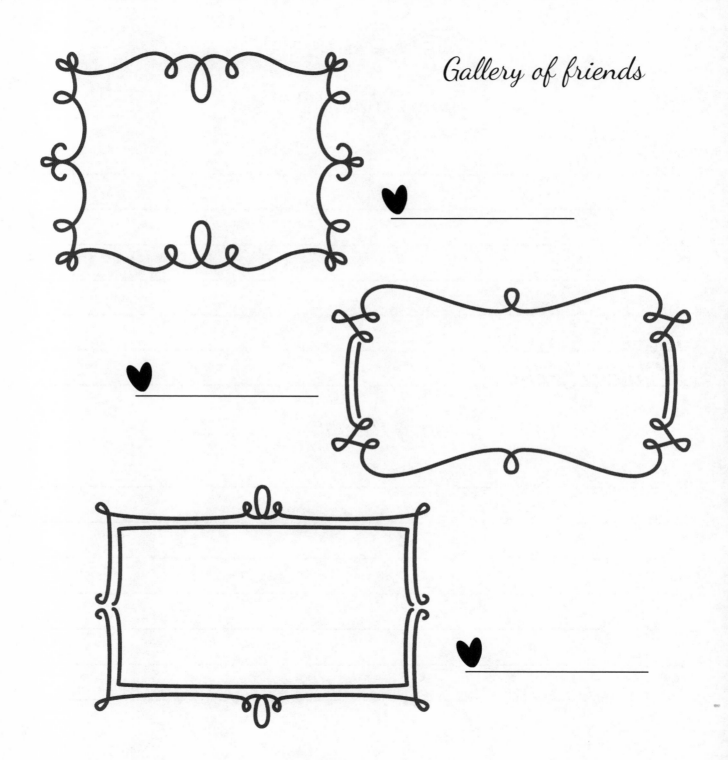

Gallery of friends

Happy thoughts......

_____

_____

_____

_____

<u>*Name*</u>

♥ <u>*Email/Phone*</u>

Happy thoughts......

_____

_____

_____

_____

<u>*Name*</u>

♥ <u>*Email/Phone*</u>

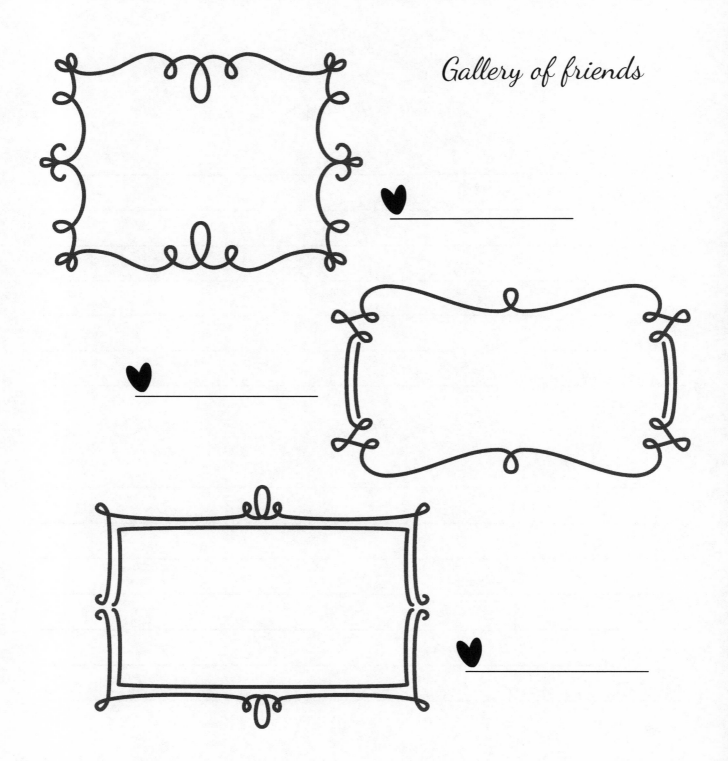

Gallery of friends

Happy thoughts......

_____

_____

_____

_____

<u>Name</u>_____

♥ *Email/Phone*_____

Happy thoughts......

_____

_____

_____

_____

<u>Name</u>_____

♥ *Email/Phone*_____

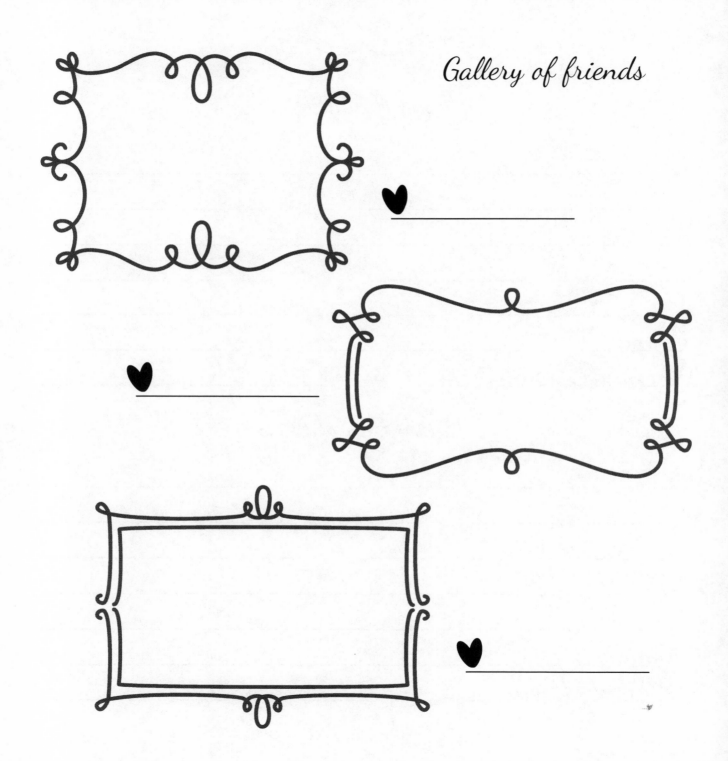

Gallery of friends

Happy thoughts......

_____

_____

_____

_____

_____

<u>Name</u>_____

♥ *Email/Phone*_____

Happy thoughts......

_____

_____

_____

_____

_____

<u>Name</u>_____

♥ *Email/Phone*_____

Gallery of friends

Happy thoughts......

_____

_____

_____

_____

_Name_____

♥ _Email/Phone_____

Happy thoughts......

_____

_____

_____

_____

_Name_____

♥ _Email/Phone_____

Gallery of friends

Happy thoughts......

_____

_____

_____

_____

_____

Name _____

♥ *Email/Phone* _____

Happy thoughts......

_____

_____

_____

_____

_____

Name _____

♥ *Email/Phone* _____

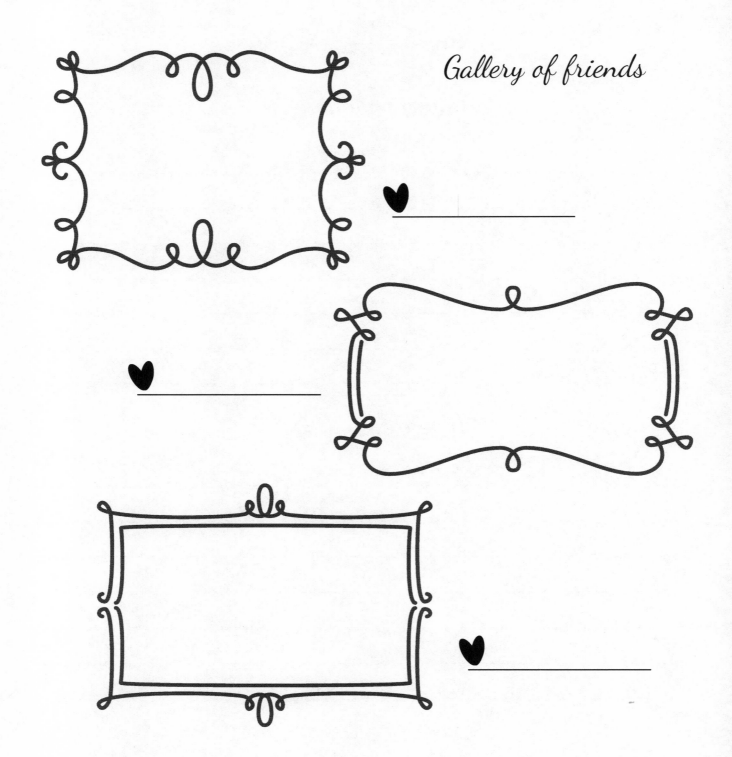

Gallery of friends

Happy thoughts......

_____

_____

_____

_____

Name _____

♥ _Email/Phone_ _____

Happy thoughts......

_____

_____

_____

_____

Name _____

♥ _Email/Phone_ _____

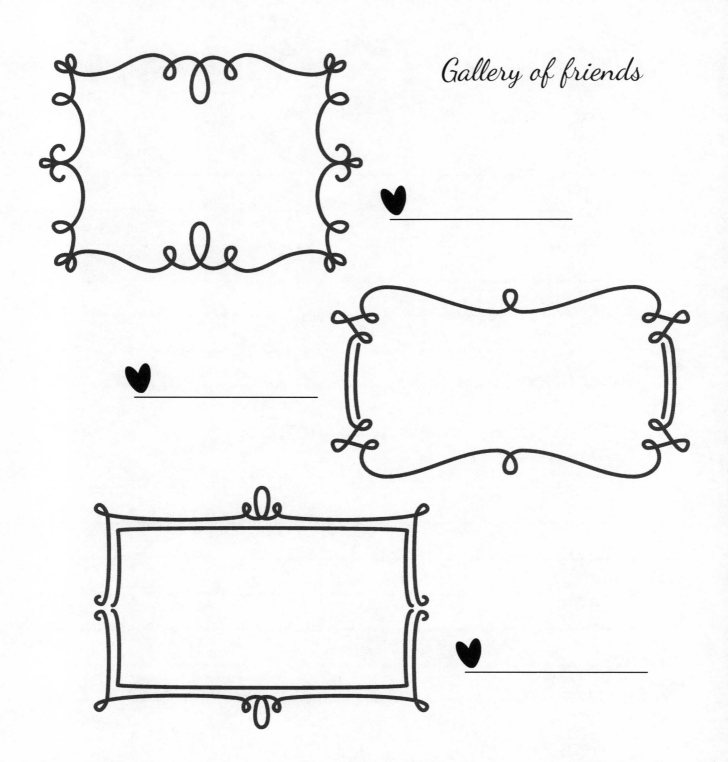

Gallery of friends

Happy thoughts......

_____

_____

_____

_____

_____

<u>*Name*</u>

♥ *Email/Phone*

Happy thoughts......

_____

_____

_____

_____

_____

<u>*Name*</u>

♥ *Email/Phone*

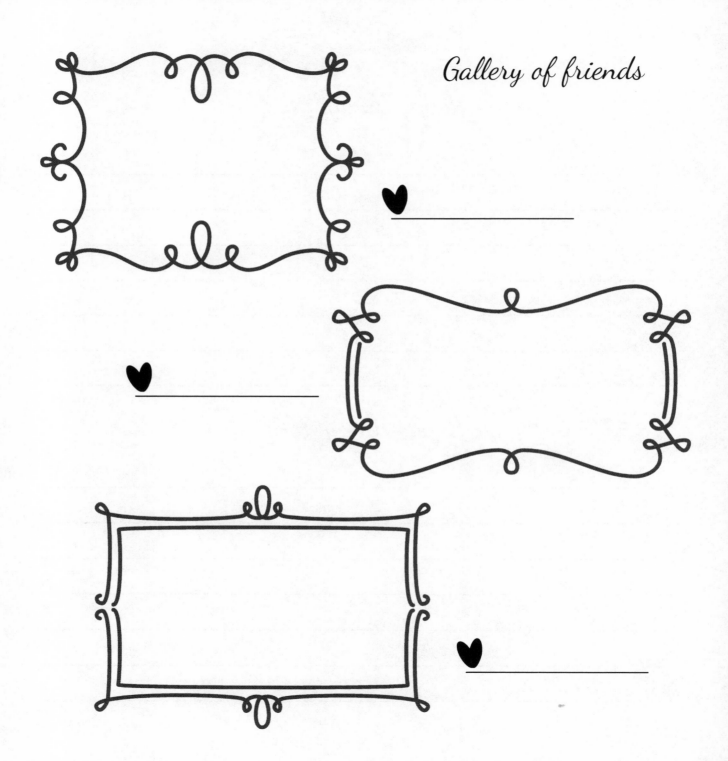

Gallery of friends

Happy thoughts......

_____

_____

_____

_____

<u>Name</u> _____

♥ *Email/Phone* _____

Happy thoughts......

_____

_____

_____

_____

<u>Name</u> _____

♥ *Email/Phone* _____

Gallery of friends

Happy thoughts......

_____

_____

_____

_____

<u>Name</u>

♥ <u>Email/Phone</u>

Happy thoughts......

_____

_____

_____

_____

<u>Name</u>

♥ <u>Email/Phone</u>

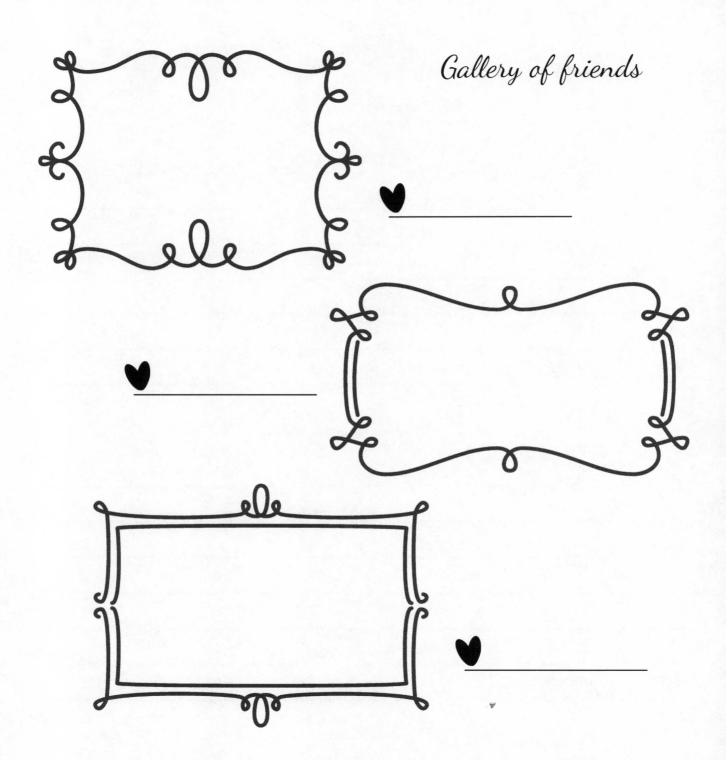

Gallery of friends

Happy thoughts......

_____
_____
_____
_____
_____

<u>Name</u> _____
♥ *Email/Phone* _____

Happy thoughts......

_____
_____
_____
_____
_____

<u>Name</u> _____
♥ *Email/Phone* _____

Gallery of friends

Happy thoughts......

_____

_____

_____

_____

Name _____

♥ *Email/Phone* _____

Happy thoughts......

_____

_____

_____

_____

Name _____

♥ *Email/Phone* _____

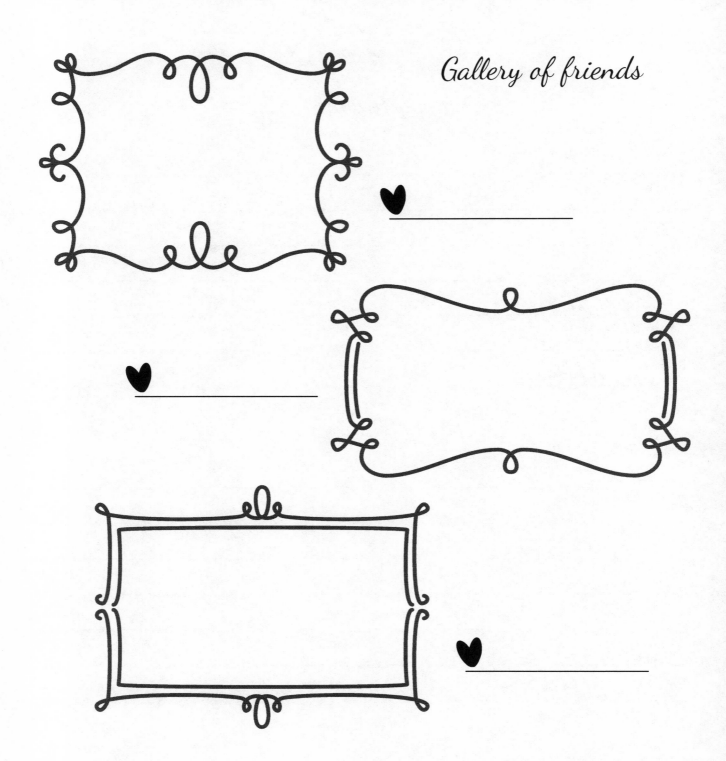

Gallery of friends

Happy thoughts......

_____

_____

_____

_____

_____

Name _____

♥ *Email/Phone* _____

Happy thoughts......

_____

_____

_____

_____

_____

Name _____

♥ *Email/Phone* _____

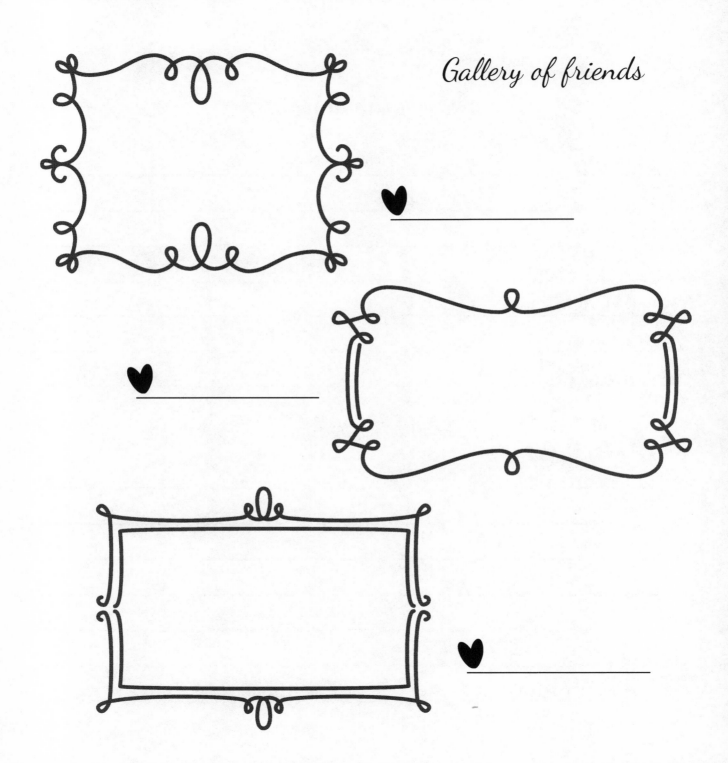

Gallery of friends

Happy thoughts......

_____

_____

_____

_____

Name

♥ *Email/Phone*

Happy thoughts......

_____

_____

_____

_____

Name

♥ *Email/Phone*

Gallery of friends

Happy thoughts......

_____

_____

_____

_____

Name _____

♥ _Email/Phone_ _____

Happy thoughts......

_____

_____

_____

_____

Name _____

♥ _Email/Phone_ _____

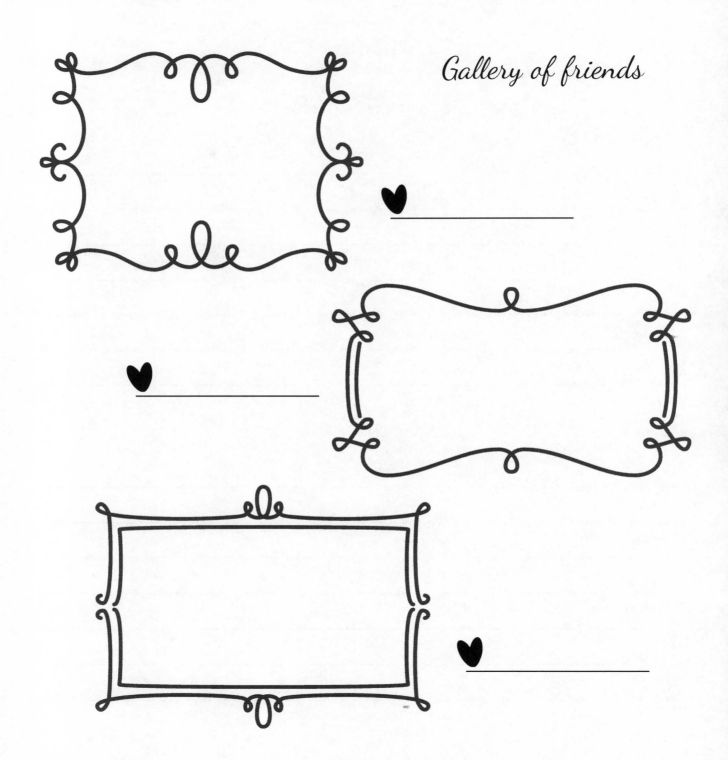

Gallery of friends

Happy thoughts......

_____

_____

_____

_____

Name _____

♥ *Email/Phone* _____

Happy thoughts......

_____

_____

_____

_____

Name _____

♥ *Email/Phone* _____

Gallery of friends

Happy thoughts......

_____

_____

_____

_____

_____

Name _____

♥ Email/Phone _____

Happy thoughts......

_____

_____

_____

_____

_____

Name _____

♥ Email/Phone _____

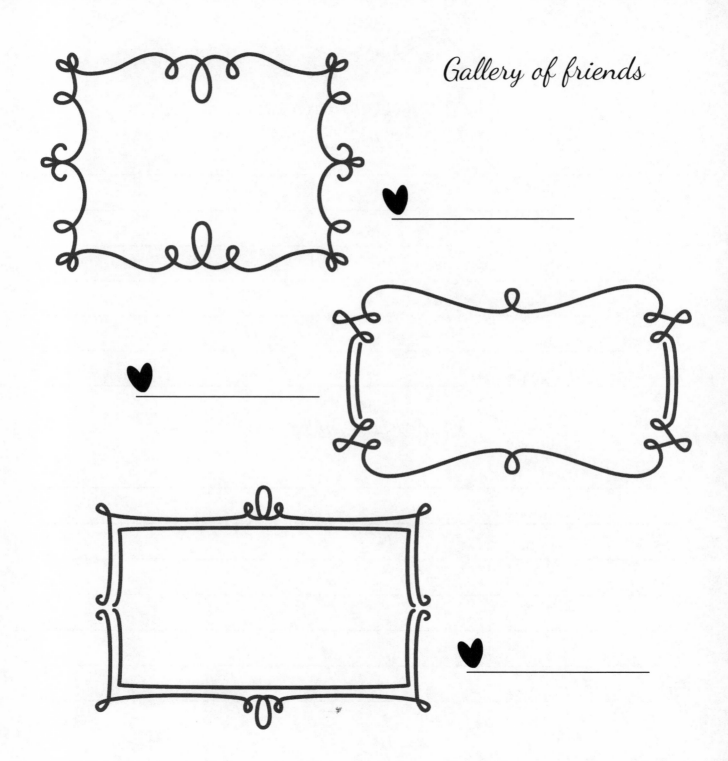

Gallery of friends

Happy thoughts......

_____

_____

_____

_____

_____

<u>Name</u>

♥ <u>Email/Phone</u>

Happy thoughts......

_____

_____

_____

_____

<u>Name</u>

♥ <u>Email/Phone</u>

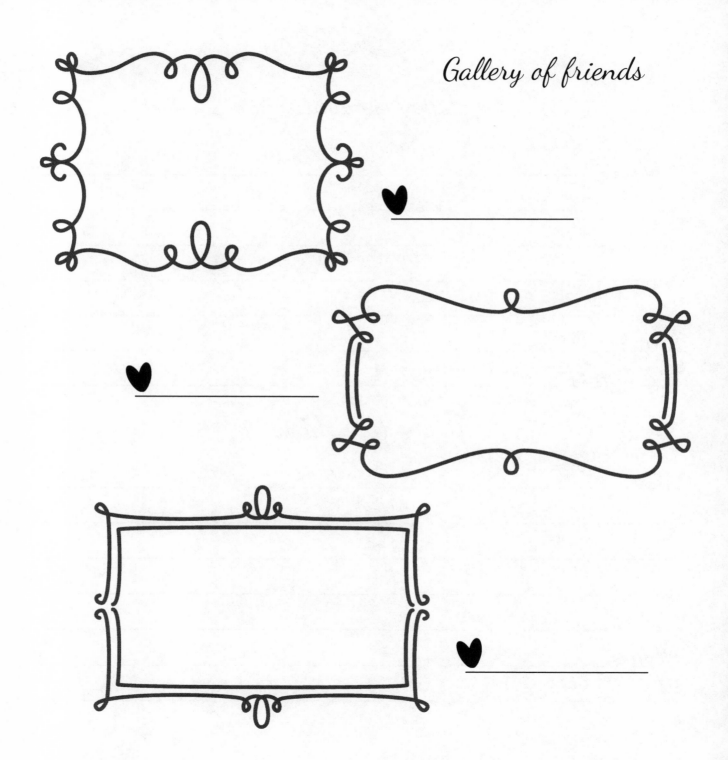

Gallery of friends

Happy thoughts......

_____

_____

_____

_____

Name

♥ Email/Phone

Happy thoughts......

_____

_____

_____

_____

Name

♥ Email/Phone

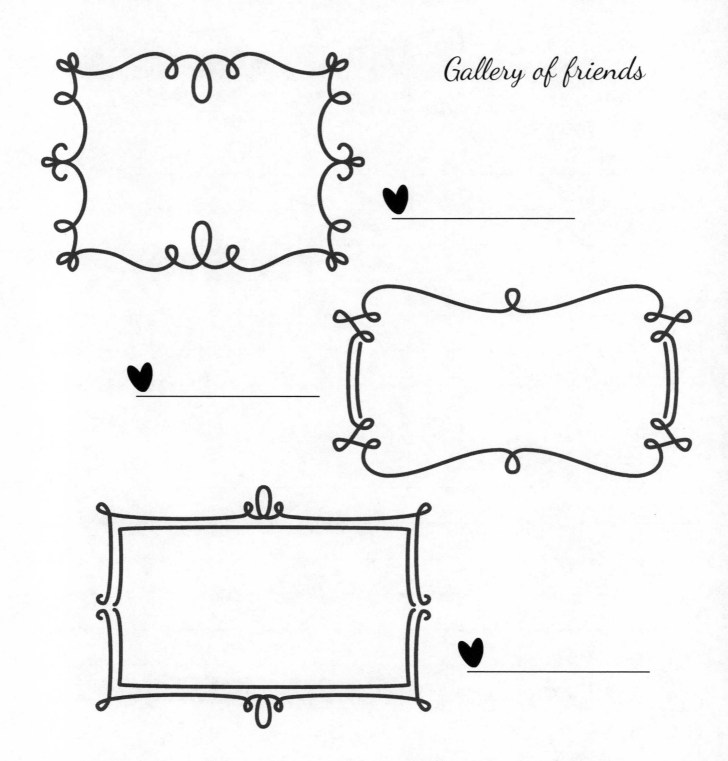

Gallery of friends

Happy thoughts......

_____

_____

_____

_____

_____

<u>Name</u>_____

♥ *Email/Phone*_____

Happy thoughts......

_____

_____

_____

_____

_____

<u>Name</u>_____

♥ *Email/Phone*_____

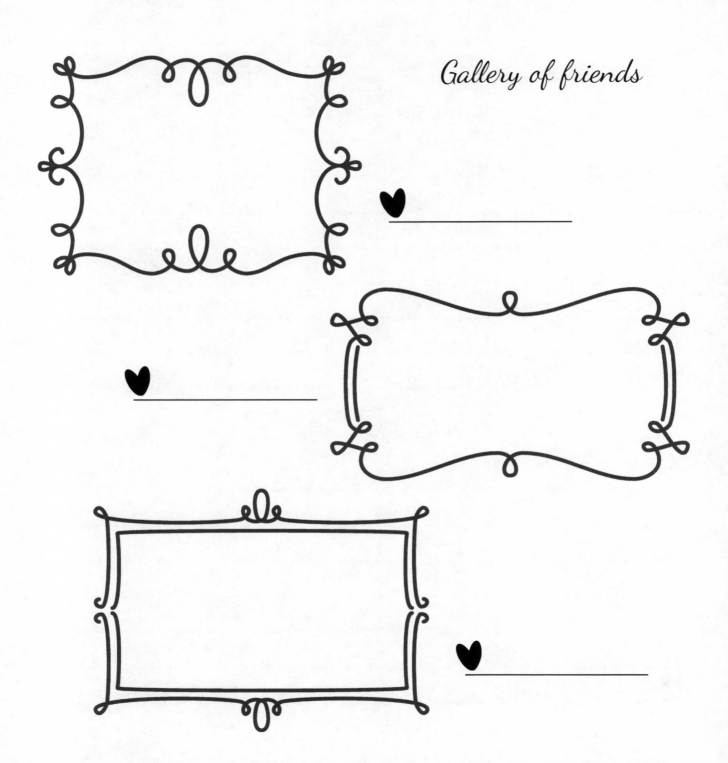

Gallery of friends

Happy thoughts......

_____

_____

_____

_____

Name _____

♥ *Email/Phone* _____

Happy thoughts......

_____

_____

_____

_____

Name _____

♥ *Email/Phone* _____

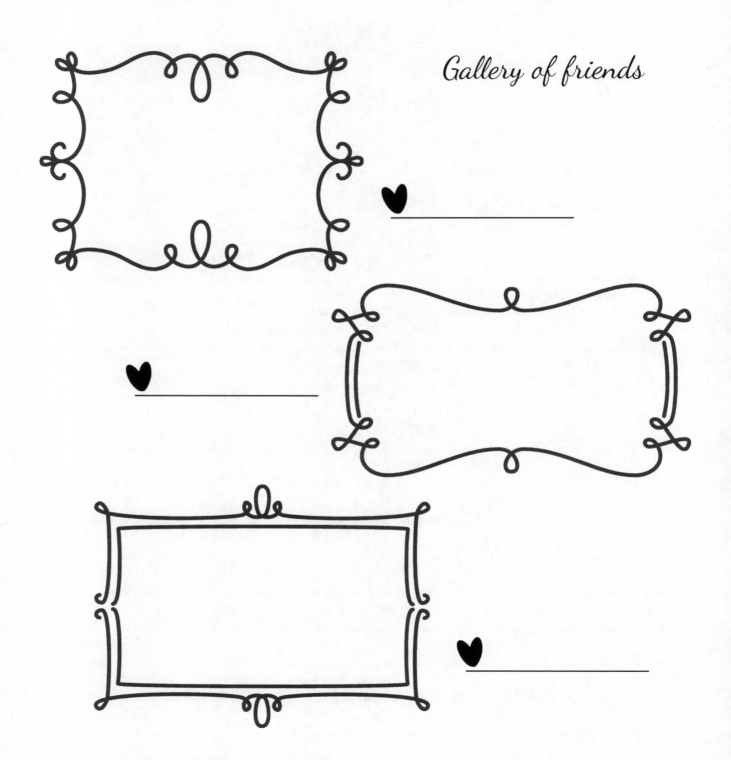

Gallery of friends

Happy thoughts......

_____

_____

_____

_____

<u>Name</u>

♥ <u>Email/Phone</u>

Happy thoughts......

_____

_____

_____

_____

<u>Name</u>

♥ <u>Email/Phone</u>

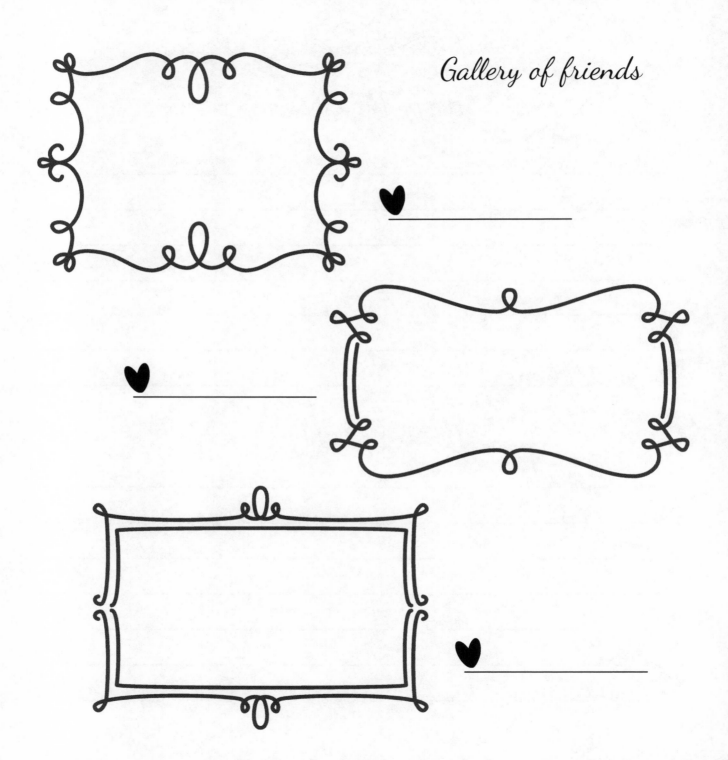

Gallery of friends

Happy thoughts......

_____

_____

_____

_____

<u>Name</u> _____

♥ *Email/Phone* _____

Happy thoughts......

_____

_____

_____

_____

<u>Name</u> _____

♥ *Email/Phone* _____

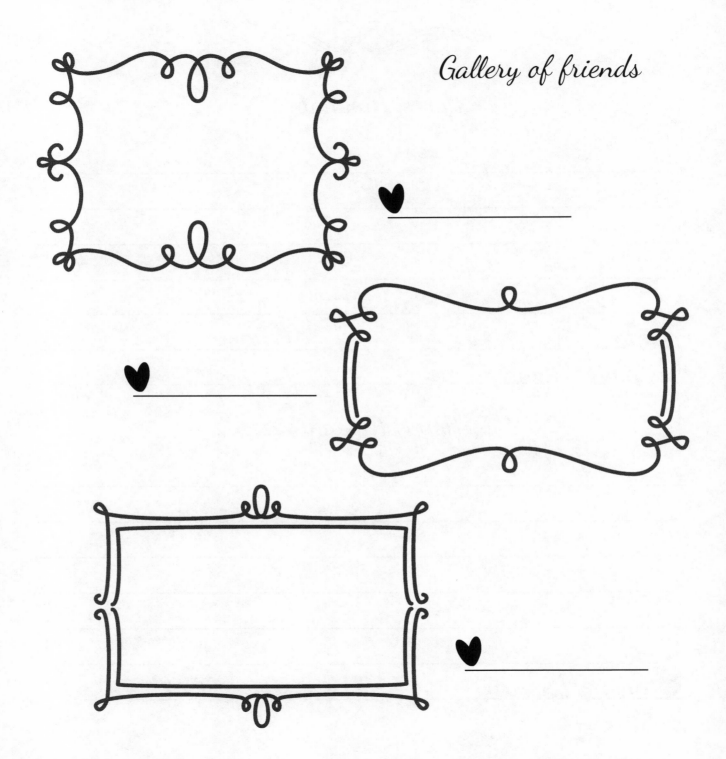

Gallery of friends

Happy thoughts......

_____

_____

_____

_____

<u>Name</u>

♥ <u>Email/Phone</u>

_____

Happy thoughts......

_____

_____

_____

_____

<u>Name</u>

♥ <u>Email/Phone</u>

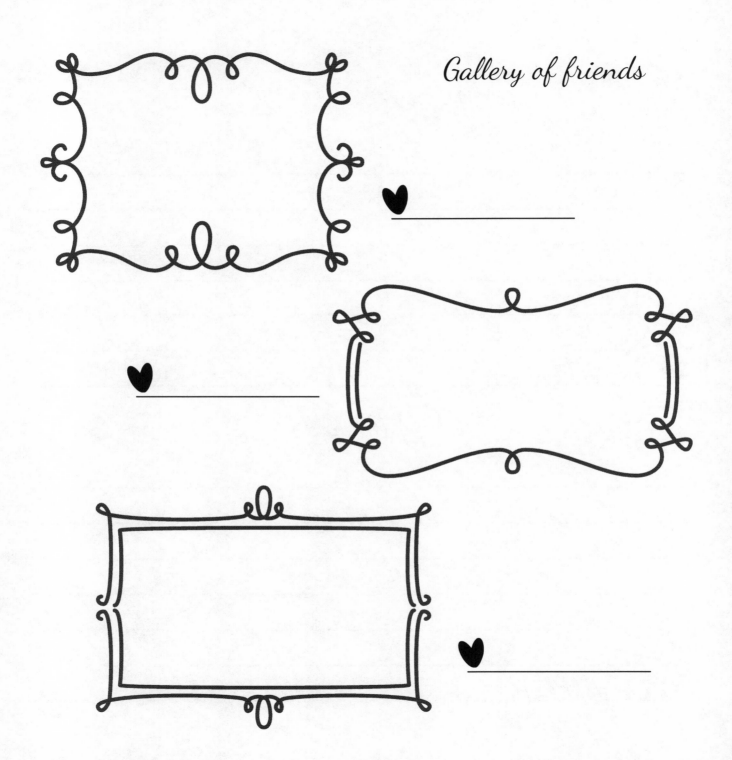

Gallery of friends

Happy thoughts......

_____

_____

_____

_____

<u>Name</u>

♥ *Email/Phone*

Happy thoughts......

_____

_____

_____

_____

<u>Name</u>

♥ *Email/Phone*

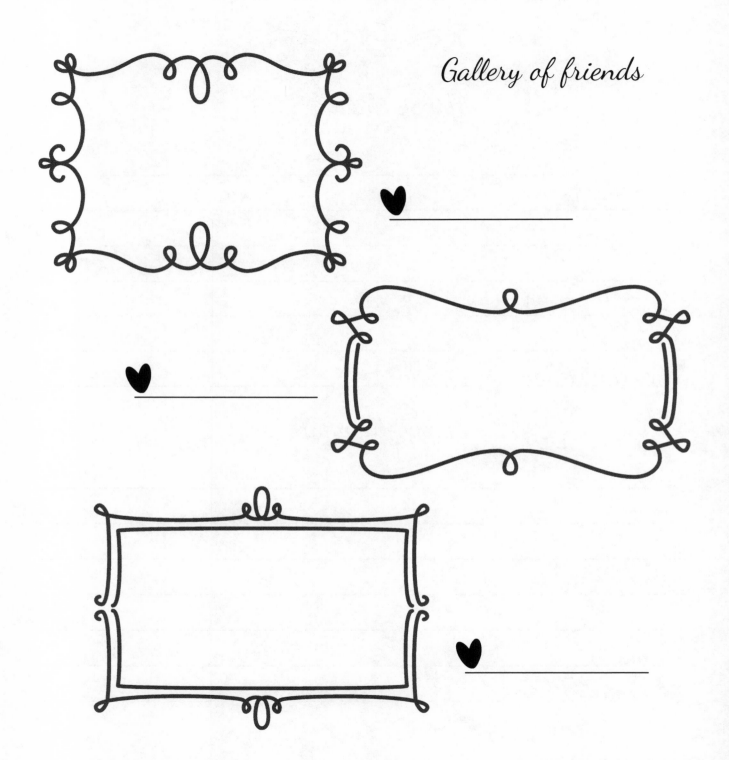

Gallery of friends

Happy thoughts......

_____

_____

_____

_____

Name

♥ *Email/Phone*

Happy thoughts......

_____

_____

_____

_____

Name

♥ *Email/Phone*

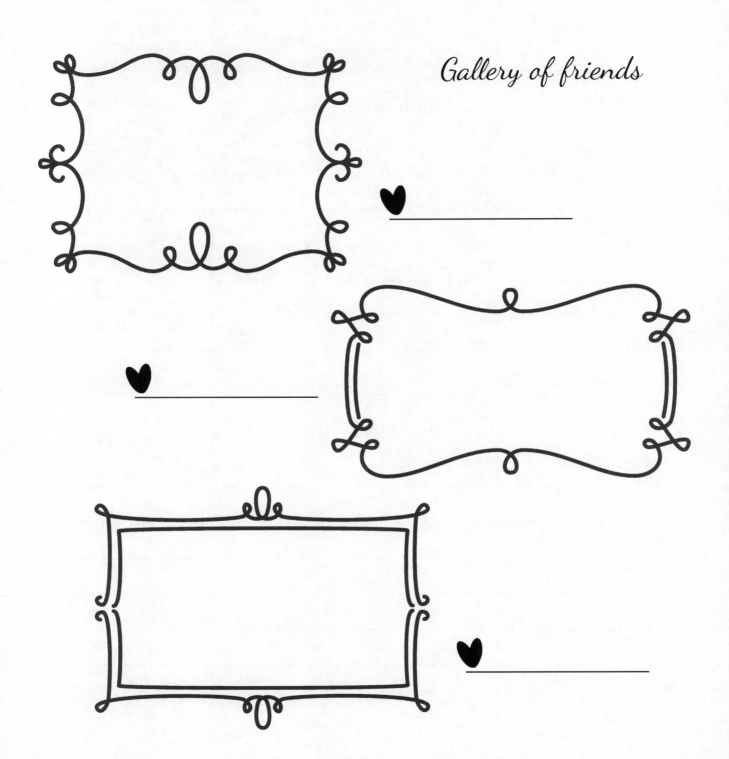

Gallery of friends

Happy thoughts......

_____

_____

_____

_____

_____

Name _____

♥ Email/Phone _____

Happy thoughts......

_____

_____

_____

_____

_____

Name _____

♥ Email/Phone _____

Gallery of friends

Happy thoughts......

_____

_____

_____

_____

_____

<u>Name</u> _____

♥ *Email/Phone* _____

Happy thoughts......

_____

_____

_____

_____

_____

<u>Name</u> _____

♥ *Email/Phone* _____

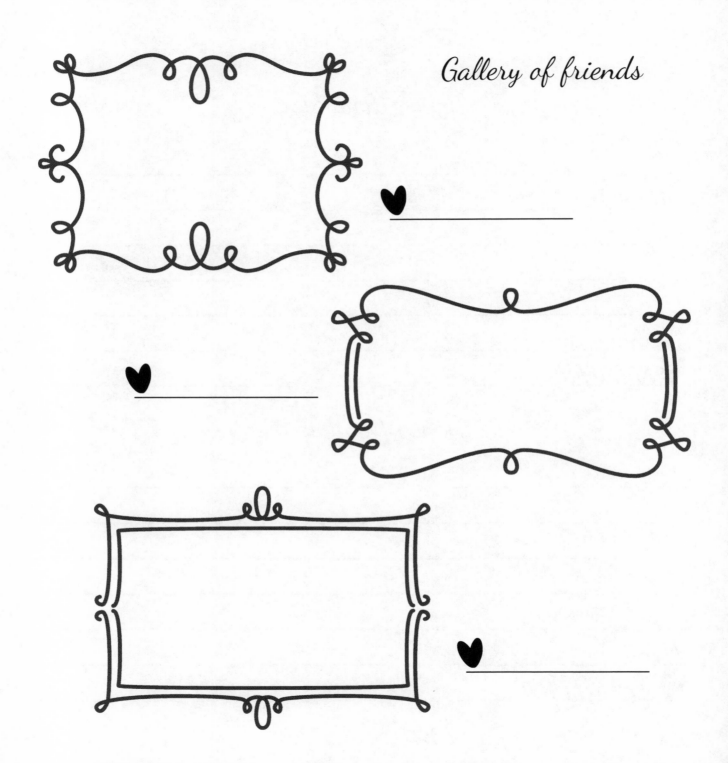

Gallery of friends

Happy thoughts......

_____

_____

_____

_____

_____

<u>Name</u>_____

♥ Email/Phone_____

Happy thoughts......

_____

_____

_____

_____

_____

<u>Name</u>_____

♥ Email/Phone_____

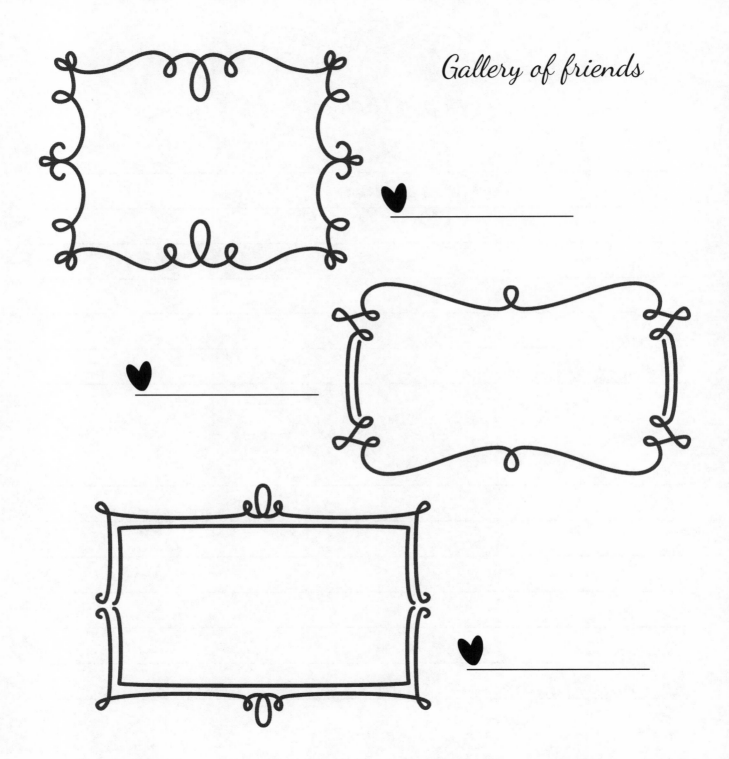

Gallery of friends

Happy thoughts......

_____

_____

_____

_____

_____

<u>Name</u>
_____
♥ <u>Email/Phone</u>
_____

Happy thoughts......

_____

_____

_____

_____

_____

<u>Name</u>
_____
♥ <u>Email/Phone</u>
_____

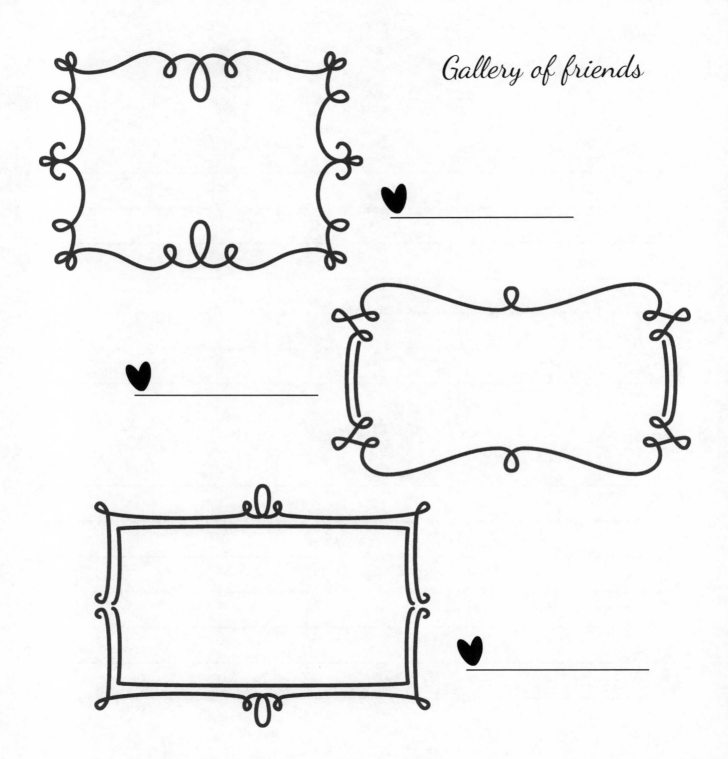

Gallery of friends

Happy thoughts......

_____

_____

_____

_____

_____

<u>Name</u>_____

♥ <u>Email/Phone</u>_____

Happy thoughts......

_____

_____

_____

_____

_____

<u>Name</u>_____

♥ <u>Email/Phone</u>_____

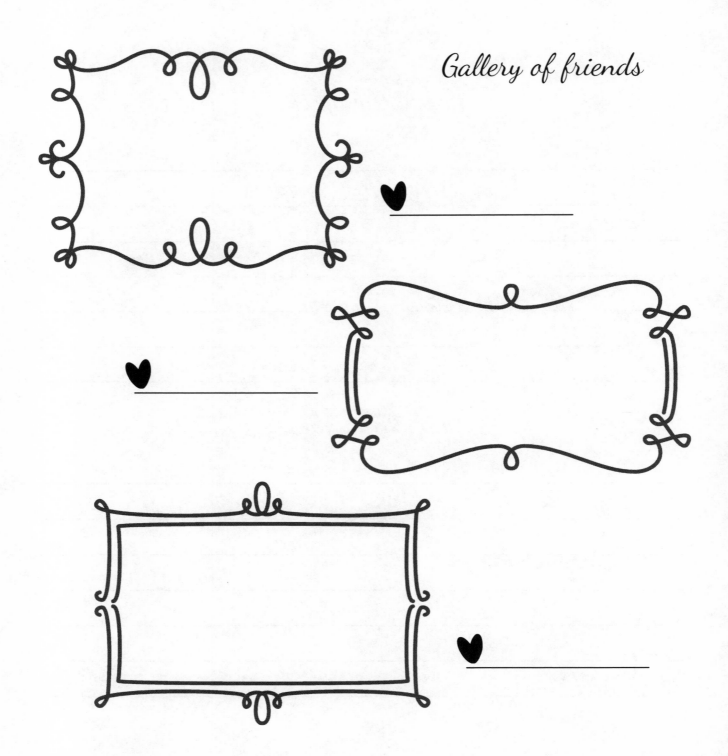

Gallery of friends

Happy thoughts......

_____

_____

_____

_____

_____

Name _____

♥ *Email/Phone* _____

Happy thoughts......

_____

_____

_____

_____

Name _____

♥ *Email/Phone* _____

Gallery of friends

Happy thoughts......

_____

_____

_____

_____

_____

Name

♥ *Email/Phone* _____

Happy thoughts......

_____

_____

_____

_____

Name

♥ *Email/Phone*

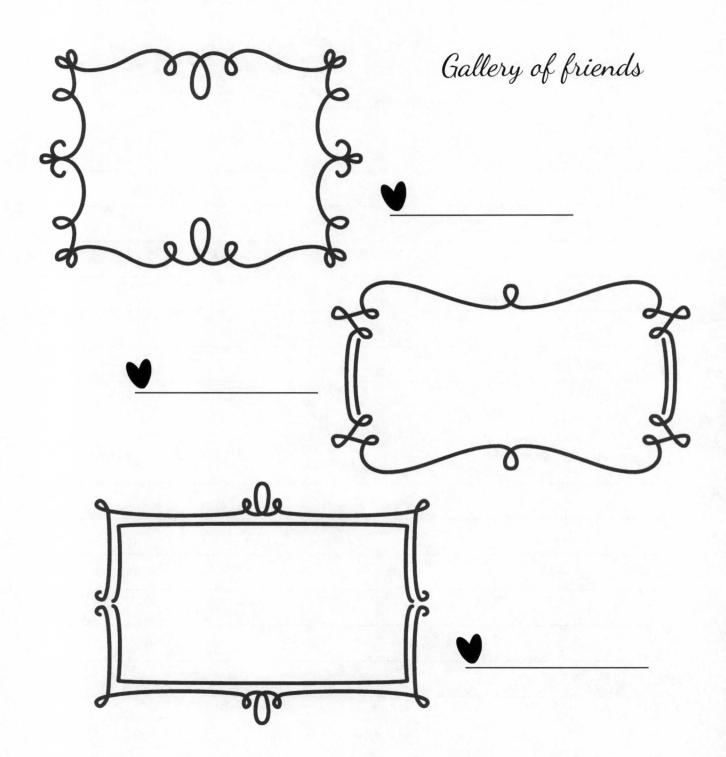

Gallery of friends

Happy thoughts......

_____

_____

_____

_____

Name _____

♥ *Email/Phone* _____

Happy thoughts......

_____

_____

_____

_____

Name _____

♥ *Email/Phone* _____

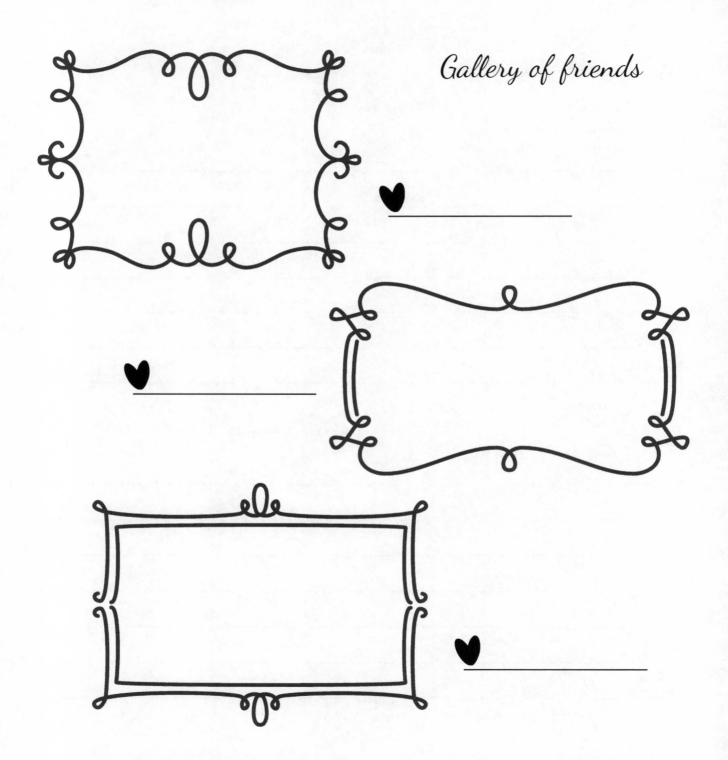

Gallery of friends

Happy thoughts......

_____

_____

_____

_____

<u>Name</u> _____

♥ <u>Email/Phone</u> _____

Happy thoughts......

_____

_____

_____

_____

<u>Name</u> _____

♥ <u>Email/Phone</u> _____

Gallery of friends

Happy thoughts......

_____

_____

_____

_____

_____

Name _____

♥ *Email/Phone* _____

Happy thoughts......

_____

_____

_____

_____

_____

Name _____

♥ *Email/Phone* _____

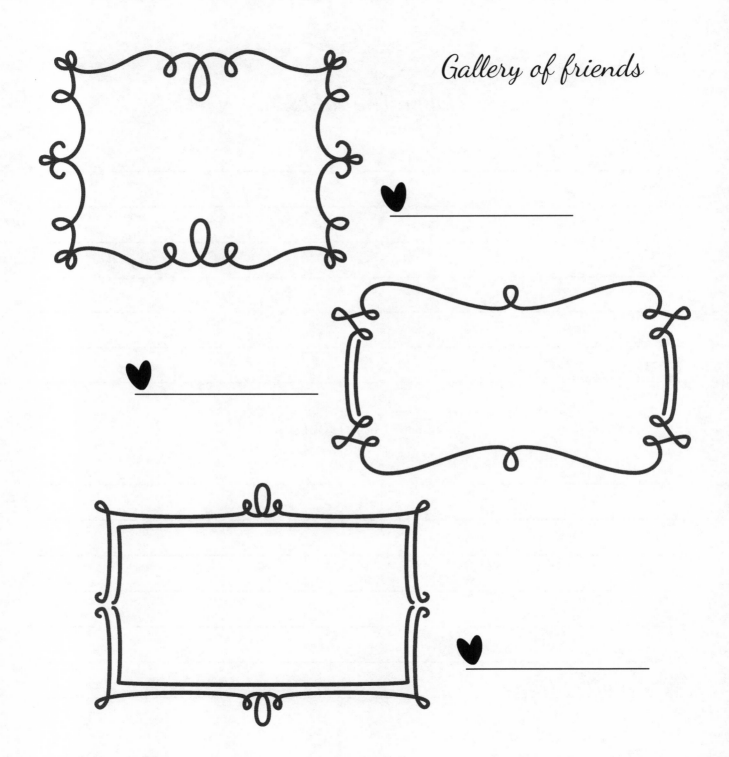

Gallery of friends

Happy thoughts......

_____

_____

_____

_____

<u>Name</u>_____

♥ <u>Email/Phone</u>_____

Happy thoughts......

_____

_____

_____

_____

<u>Name</u>_____

♥ <u>Email/Phone</u>_____

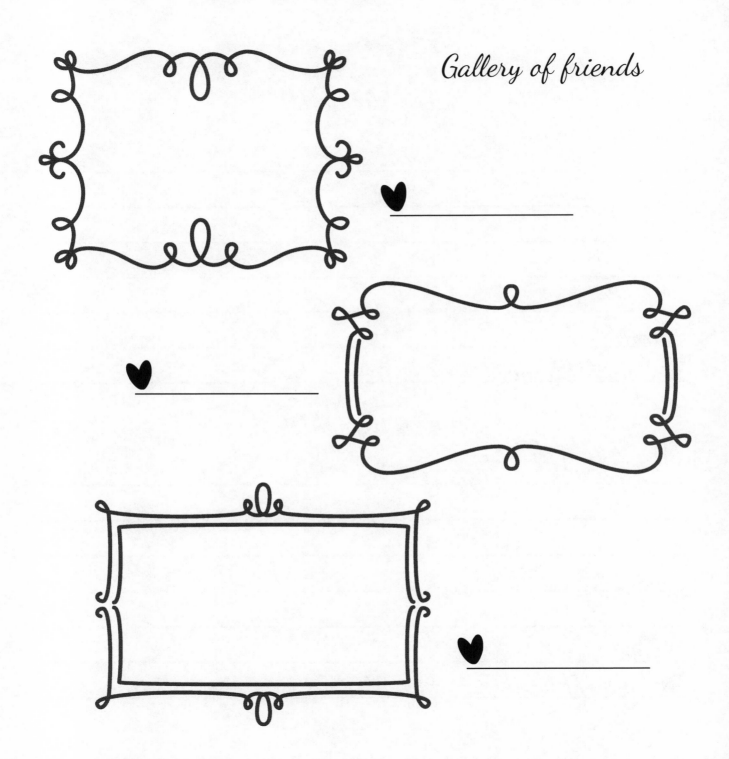

Gallery of friends

Happy thoughts......

_____

_____

_____

_____

<u>Name</u>_____

♥ <u>Email/Phone</u>_____

Happy thoughts......

_____

_____

_____

_____

<u>Name</u>_____

♥ <u>Email/Phone</u>_____

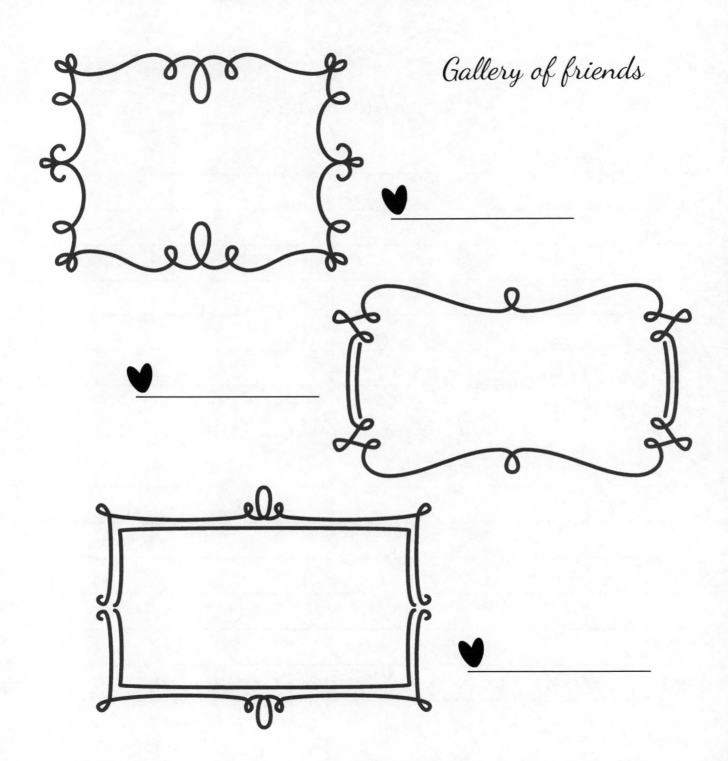

Gallery of friends

Happy thoughts......

_____

_____

_____

_____

<u>Name</u>

♥ <u>Email/Phone</u>

Happy thoughts......

_____

_____

_____

_____

<u>Name</u>

♥ <u>Email/Phone</u>

Gallery of friends

Happy thoughts......

_____

_____

_____

_____

_____

<u>Name</u>

♥ <u>Email/Phone</u>

Happy thoughts......

_____

_____

_____

_____

_____

<u>Name</u>

♥ <u>Email/Phone</u>

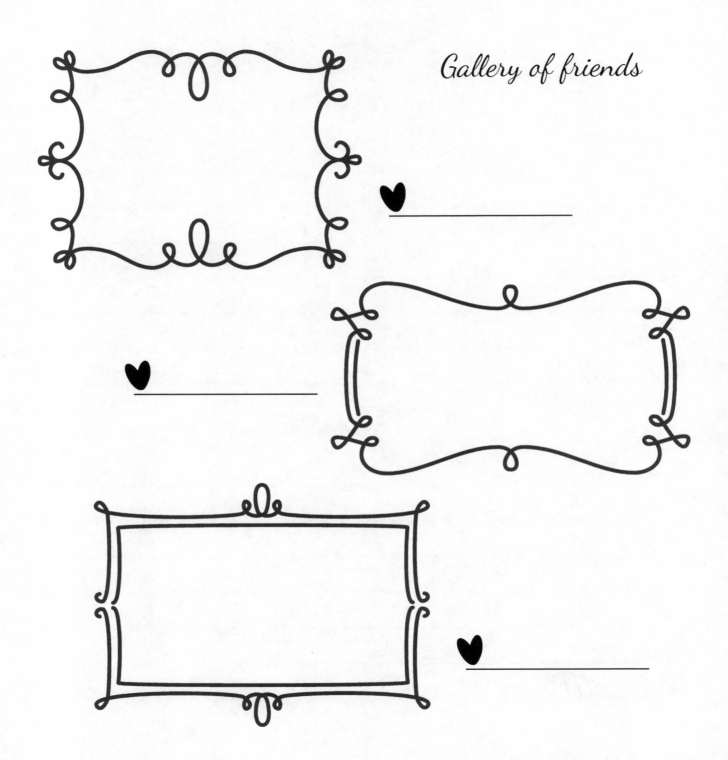

Gallery of friends

Happy thoughts......

_____

_____

_____

_____

<u>Name</u>

♥ <u>Email/Phone</u>

Happy thoughts......

_____

_____

_____

_____

<u>Name</u>

♥ <u>Email/Phone</u>

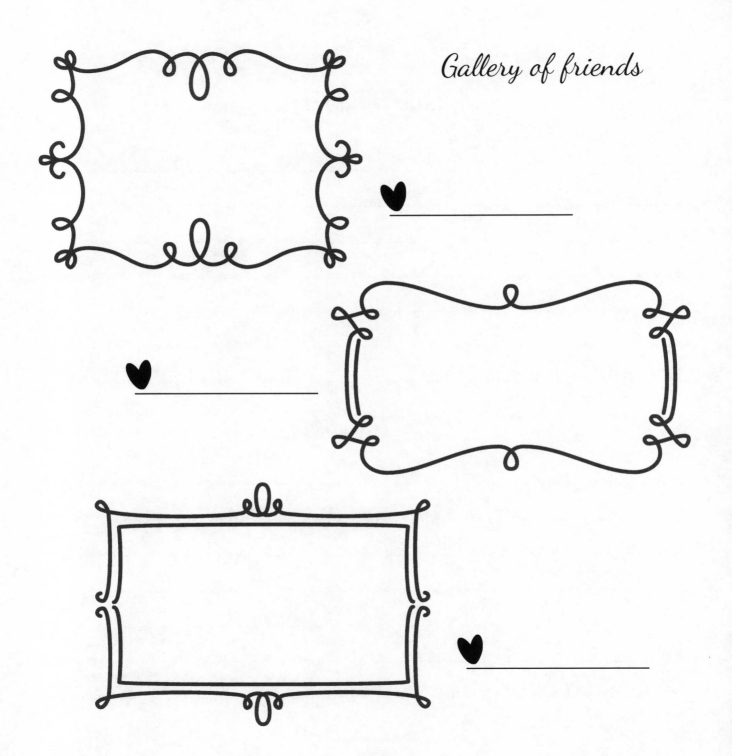

Gallery of friends

Happy thoughts......

_____

_____

_____

_____

<u>*Name*</u>

♥ *Email/Phone*
_____

Happy thoughts......

_____

_____

_____

_____

<u>*Name*</u>

♥ *Email/Phone*
_____

Gallery of friends

Happy thoughts......

_____

_____

_____

_____

<u>Name</u>

♥ <u>Email/Phone</u>

Happy thoughts......

_____

_____

_____

_____

<u>Name</u>

♥ <u>Email/Phone</u>

Gallery of friends

Happy thoughts......

_____

_____

_____

_____

Name _____

♥ *Email/Phone* _____

Happy thoughts......

_____

_____

_____

_____

Name _____

♥ *Email/Phone* _____

Gift from	Thank you note sent

Gift from	Thank you note sent

Gift from	Thank you note sent

Gift from	Thank you note sent

Gift from	Thank you note sent

Gift from	Thank you note sent

Gift from	Thank you note sent

Gift from	Thank you note sent

Made in the USA
San Bernardino, CA
16 July 2019